Leisure Arts 9

Painting Detail in Watercolour

Richard Bolton

Search Press, London
Taplinger Publishing Co., New York
A Pentalic Book
Methuen, Sydney

Introduction

Watercolour is difficult to master but a good medium in which to learn how to paint as it encourages you to use paint confidently and accurately. This is partly because once you have made a mistake you cannot cover it up: you just have to start again.

The best way to improve your technique and style in painting is to practise as much as possible. Studying books and advice from teachers never give the same results. The old saying 'you learn by your mistakes' is particularly appropriate to watercolour: a great deal of patience and self-control is needed to analyze an error, especially if you have just ruined a good painting with a couple of careless brushstrokes.

All these difficulties are easily offset by the excitement of trying to capture light and luminosity in watercolour and the satisfaction of obtaining good results fairly quickly. A sky, for instance, can be painted in moments, whereas with oils it can take days. Watercolour is clean and economical; you need no more than a box of paints and a couple of brushes. For oil painting, however, you need much more equipment and you will probably make your house or studio smell of turpentine.

Throughout this book I show my own way of painting. Nevertheless, I realize that other artists may have different techniques, and I believe that if a technique works you should use it. This premise is borne out by the work of such masters of watercolour as Turner and Sargent, who used any method that they thought would have the right effect.

I hope my demonstrations will encourage you to use watercolour with control and confidence – factors which make it the most challenging and rewarding of all painting media.

Great Gransden windmill

This deserted old post-windmill is exactly the kind of subject that excites me. It has broken lines and blotchy areas of colour that demand a sharp and contrasting treatment. The scene breaks down into three main parts; the windmill needs drybrush and wet into dry to make it stand out as the focal point; the foreground calls for wet into wet to give soft edges to the mass of undergrowth; and the trees lack any definite colour but give shape to the painting. I have left out a road that runs to the right as I felt it detracted from the windmill and impaired the overall composition.

Demonstration

Size: 355 × 254 mm/14 × 10 in. Paper: T H Saunders NOT 180gsm/90lb. Brushes: Chinese bamboo no. 9, 1 sable, flat sable. Colours used: cadmium orange, cadmium red, cadmium yellow, bright red, cobalt blue.

Stage 1

Make a simple drawing of the principal subjects. This is a relatively easy scene to draw as there are no ellipses or complicated details. Do not try to draw each plank of wood of the windmill but create an overall impression with broken lines. Apply masking fluid to the posts in the foreground to produce hard edges and make them stand out sharply against the mass of foliage. I usually begin by painting the background and work forward and this is what I have done here. Choose a simple sky that does not detract from the subject. Mix plenty of paint and lay in a gentle wash, working from side to side. When you get halfway down the sky, add more water to thin the paint as the paler colour will give distance to the horizon. If you raise the top of the board a little, the wash will bead along the working edge and give an interesting line. Let the sky dry.

Stage 2

The near side of the windmill is made entirely of planks of wood and these provide the greatest challenge in this painting. With watercolour it is possible to create the illusion of planks of wood without actually painting each one. If you try to paint each plank you will lose the freedom which is the hallmark of watercolour painting. Paint the planks by using the side of a moist brush and make quick strokes across the rough paper surface, so that the paint does not reach the hollows of the paper. Practise this technique until you have exactly

Stage 1

Stage 2

Stage 3

Stage 4

the right amount of paint on the brush. If you overload the brush, too much paint will be shed on the paper and you will lose the uneven, speckled effect. Give some thought to each brushstroke as remedies are rarely satisfactory and will produce a heavy, muddy texture.

Stage 3

Complete the windmill by adding heavy shadow on one side and under a few of the planks to give texture. Put in the line of trees to the left of the horizon using pure cobalt blue. Before the paint dries, run a wet brush along the bottom edge of the trees to blend off the colour.

Stage 4

The big problem with the two large trees in the foreground is to avoid hard edges which occur when the paint dries out. Work upwards from the base of the tree. First soften the bottom edge with a damp brush,

Stage 5 – the finished painting

then work upwards with a well-loaded brush. This prevents the paint from drying out too quickly and enables you to move from one branch to another keeping all the edges wet. Keep the colour subdued so that the trees are not too dominant. Finish off the twigs with a fine no. 1 sable brush.

Stage 5

Complete the foreground with great care. Wet the paper on the left and work in diluted colours, letting them diffuse into one another. Do not push the paint around too much or it will end up looking muddy. Wet some of the area on the right to create patches of white with hard edges. The soft, wet edges of all the undergrowth provide a good contrast to the stark outlines of the windmill. Paint some grasses and posts just below the windmill on to dry paper. Finally rub away the masking fluid on the posts, give them texture with drybrush and highlight them with shadow.

Drawing

In my opinion, your watercolour painting will be unsuccessful if you do not develop your drawing skill, for good drawing is the foundation on which to build your painting. The only way to improve it is to practise constantly. Ideally, you should try to draw something every day. It does not matter what you draw so long as you work from life. Draw articles in the home, or when out walking, bring back shells, pieces of bark from trees and any interesting objects. Your main aim is to produce accurate drawings. It is easy for a beginner to be content with a superficial likeness of a subject, but improvement comes only from continually analyzing your drawing, no matter how experienced you are, and by developing a strongly critical approach to your work.

It is useful to keep a sketchbook so that you can look back over your work to see your mistakes and improvements. You will find that drawings that pleased you in the past no longer satisfy you. Try not to waste pages in your sketchbook; use each page fully and always finish each drawing.

Joining art classes can be a great help in working out ideas and encouraging you to improve your technique. Visit galleries and read art books as these can often be good sources of inspiration. Try to build up a small library of your own.

For watercolour painting all you need is a simple, accurate line drawing to guide you in your painting. I use an HB pencil for all my drawing, as hard pencils scar the paper and soft ones leave too heavy a line. Occasionally it is useful to have strong lines in your painting, for example in an architectural subject that has many straight lines. Keep your pencil sharp and try to produce clear, crisp line work. Avoid using a sketchy technique that leaves ugly feathery lines, and always try to make a drawing with as few lines as possible.

Paint

It is best to buy artist quality paints from the start if you can afford them. I prefer pans because they are very compact and enable me to paint outside with the minimum of equipment. A brush cannot pick up so much colour from a pan as from a tube, but pans prevent the over-use of colour, and encourage luminosity and the use of white paper for highlights.

A wide range of colours is not necessary and the average paint box has more than enough colour slots. Buy full pans of colour.

I often change the contents of my paint box, depending on the colours that I favour at the time. You need little science to choose or position colours, but you must try to keep various colours in groups: eg. reds on one corner, blues in another. Yellows are always difficult to keep clean and they usually end up looking green.

Some of my favourite colours that I use very often are: cobalt blue, Prussian blue, cadmium orange, cadmium red, cadmium yellow and bright red.

The old Ford

I found this old car rotting away in an abandoned quarry. It was particularly appealing to me as I owned one just like it years ago.

The great challenge of this subject was to capture its dilapidated state, the green mould growing over the paintwork and the rust appearing where the paint had come away. Vandals had bent the doors and smashed the glass, providing me with a superb subject to paint.

Demonstration

Size: 370 × 266 mm/14½ × 10½ in. Paper: T H Saunders NOT 180gsm/90lb. Brushes: Chinese bamboo no. 9, 1 sable. Colours used; cadmium red, cadmium yellow, French ultramarine, yellow ochre, cobalt blue.

Stage 1

After drawing the subject, apply masking fluid to the branches in front of the vehicle and the long grass that reaches up high around the car in the foreground. It is impossible to achieve these thin white lines by trying to paint round the blades of grass, or by painting them in with white paint afterwards. I left the background out altogether as it was a quarry face that did not enhance the subject at all.

Stage 2

Where you start painting the car is not really important. I began in the small corner of the front windscreen (windshield) where there were some harsh lines that allowed me to get the paints wet and to feel my way with the colours. Work towards the back of the car, filling in the darkest areas inside, using a mixture of cadmium red, cobalt blue and yellow ochre.

Stage 3

To paint the doors and body panels, use two brushes, one filled with cadmium yellow and the other charged with a mixture of cadmium red, cobalt blue and French ultramarine. The yellow gives the effect of mould growing round the base of the car. First paint in the yellow and, while it is wet, work in the mixture on the other

Stage 1

Stage 2

Stage 3

Stage 4

brush. The two colours merge together to create an effect you cannot get in any other way. Try not to overmix colours and do not stir them around on the paper more than you can help, as this only leads to a dulling of colour and a muddy effect.

Stage 4

Mix some cadmium red and yellow ochre and apply it to the interior of the car. Use yellow to suggest mould around the far door. Make up a pale green from cadmium yellow and French ultramarine and place it around the base of the car to suggest undergrowth. Blend this wash at the top with plenty of water so that the hard edges appear only below the car. When painting this car, I found there was too much dark blue around the front mudguard, so I used a little ox gall to disperse the excess colour upwards and create a better tonal balance.

Stage 5 – the finished painting

Stage 5

To complete the picture, paint patches of pale green wash into dry paper around the base of the car. Use some drybrush to give broken shapes and when dry, remove all the masking fluid from the painting. Paint the tree with a mixture of cadmium red and yellow ochre and dark blue, using drybrush to give texture to the branches. Flick in some dead brown grasses among the green undergrowth, and add a few touches of cadmium red below the windscreen (windshield).

Brushes

It is generally accepted that sable hair is the best watercolour brush because it returns to shape after each brushstroke. Ox hair brushes are cheaper than sable but do not keep their shape so well. I use Chinese bamboo brushes which look unconventional but handle extremely well and come to a fine point. I do most of my painting with this type of brush now though I still use a no. 1 sable brush for fine detail and a large 25 mm/1 in. flat brush for washes.

Always test a brush in the shop before buying it. This is not necessary with Chinese bamboo brushes as the bristles are soaked in a hardening solution to maintain their wet shape. Most art shops provide a small container of water in which to dip brushes. Select a few brushes, dip each one into the water, give one vigorous flick and pick the one with the best shape and finest point.

You will need surprisingly few brushes, but if you are like me you will eventually accumulate many of them, though you will leave some sitting in the jar and hardly ever use them. I keep some that are past their best to apply masking fluid. My favourite brushes are shown below with some of the effects they can give.

below:
My favourite brushes. Top, a 25 mm/1 in. flat sable; centre, two no. 9 Chinese bamboo brushes; below, a no. 1 sable.

Tractor and trailer: demonstration

This ancient tractor and trailer provided an interesting challenge to create textures that show the effect of years of hard use and heavy work. The original colours have faded and are mottled by smears of oil and spreading rust.

Brushstroke made by a large flat sable.

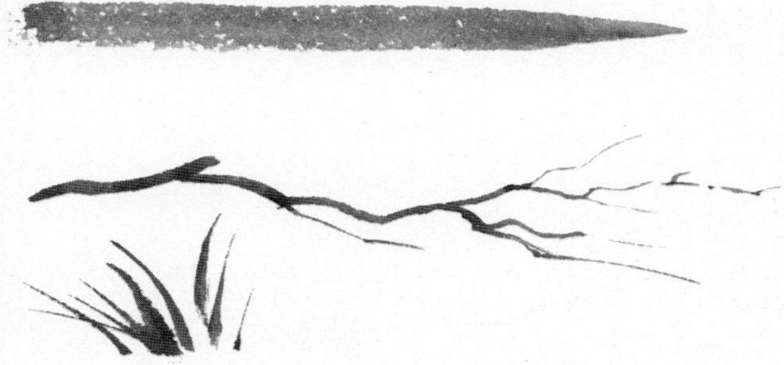

A Chinese bamboo brush produces beautiful tapering lines ideal for grass and branches.

A no. 1 sable makes all fine lines and small details.

Size: 260 × 260 mm/10¼ × 10¼ in. Paper: T H Saunders NOT 180gsm/90lb. Brushes: Chinese bamboo no. 9, 1 sable, flat sable. Colours used; cadmium orange, cadmium red, cadmium yellow, yellow ochre, burnt sienna, cobalt blue, Prussian blue, cerulean blue.

Stage 1

Drawing the ellipses in the tractor wheels is difficult; take care to draw them correctly. I usually construct an ellipse quite briskly using the natural arc created by my wrist and, if it is wrong, I simply erase it and try again.

The sky is a wash of pure cobalt blue with just a touch of burnt sienna, merging into cadmium orange and yellow ochre. Paint the hills with cobalt blue, and a mixture of the same colour, burnt sienna and yellow ochre.

Stage 2

Use a mixture of cobalt blue and burnt sienna to brush in the trees and then concentrate on the tractor. Use masking fluid to cover details such as nuts, bolts and various electrical leads around the engine. The wheels are difficult so start with one of these; it is better to

Stage 1

Stage 2

Stage 3

Stage 4

Detail of the tractor shown on the front cover

ruin the painting now than with the last few brush-strokes. Mix cobalt blue, cadmium red and cadmium yellow for the back wheel of the tractor and work round the tyre, keeping the paint wet and varying the tone. Leave white paper for the highlights on the tyre tread and add a little drybrush for the dirt on the walls of the tyre.

Now begin work on the darkest areas of the tractor. Mix Prussian blue and cadmium red for the hood, parts of the engine and the underside to give the tractor some shape.

Stage 3

The basic colour for the tractor bodywork is cerulean blue with a touch of cadmium yellow. Dab this colour on in thin washes of broken colour to produce the dilapidated effect. Paint in some burnt sienna, using drybrush to create realistic rust. Treat the radiator like a sheet of clear Perspex or a similar material by painting some vertical bars of grey and then adding a wash. If you try to paint the grill-mesh wire by wire, it will look overworked.

Use extremely pale washes on the trailer which has lost all sign of its original paint and varnish and has taken on all manner of natural colours. Complete it by adding the rusty frame and some screw heads that hold it together.

Stage 4

Give shape and form to the engine by working in brown made from burnt sienna mixed with cadmium orange, cerulean blue, Prussian blue and a few dots of light green made from cerulean blue and cadmium yellow. Put in some dark nuts and bolts on the vehicle frame, then complete the front wheels with a wash of cadmium red, cadmium yellow and cobalt blue. Do not complete the whole of each tyre, but leave the lower part unpainted.

Stage 5 (*shown on front cover*)

The dead grass around the tractor is a mauve and rust colour. Treat this very loosely, applying lots of clear water and dashing in brushfuls of paint on to dry and wet paper to produce hard and soft edges. There is always some risk when using washes in this manner, though you can soak up the first attempt with tissues and begin again – but remember that the paper will lose its crisp, white surface if you have to resort to doing this.

Finally, remove all masking fluid from nut and bolt heads and the electrical leads on the engine, and put in a *few* fine mechanical details for the sake of realism.

page 13:
Use a very loose approach when painting the engine details. Do not try to paint each item but create an overall impression of oily old mechanical parts.

opposite:
An enlarged view of the preliminary drawing on page 12. Study the line work carefully and notice how detail is kept to an absolute minimum to let the watercolour paint do all the work.

Detail of stage 1 on page 12

Detail of the barge and estuary on page 21

Detail of the teazels on page 29

Paper

Use high-quality rag paper for watercolour painting. Cheaper papers made from wood pulp turn yellow, disintegrate with age and are generally considered to be unsuitable for watercolour. All watercolour paper used to be hand-made, but now it is mostly machine-made. Fortunately, there is no noticeable drop in quality.

It is necessary to stretch all but the heaviest grades of paper to prevent cockling when a wash is applied. Stretching paper does not take long, but do it well in advance as the stretching process entails soaking and paper must be dry before you begin painting.

To stretch paper, soak it in a clean bath, let it absorb as much water as possible and then transfer it to a flat board. Place tissues on the board to keep the under surface of the paper as clean as possible, so that if the painting is unsuccessful, you can use the reverse side. Place gumstrip tape around the edge of the wet paper so that when it dries out, it pulls tight without cockling.

I keep a protective cover on my board that can be folded over either side. I stretch two pieces of paper, one on each side of the board and keep one side clean while I am painting on the other.

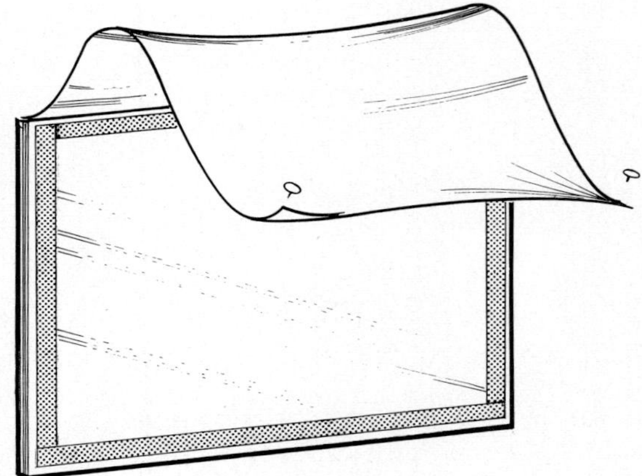

above:
Paper stretched on a board, held by gumstrip tape and protected by a cover of cotton or cheesecloth.

below:
Laying a wash. The paint beads along the lower edge of each brushstroke.

Wash technique

The purpose of a watercolour wash is to produce an even distribution of diluted paint over a large area of paper. Before laying a wash, have everything you need laid out before you. If you break off to look for paper tissues, hard edges will form where the paint dries and these cannot be removed.

When mixing a colour, test it on a piece of waste paper for the right strength. If the colour is too strong, add some more water. Make sure you have more than enough paint as you will not have time to mix more once you have started.

Tilt the top end of the board up a few degrees to make the diluted paint mixture run towards you. Take a large brush such as a 25 mm/1 in. square-ended sable, and charge it with paint. Drag the brush carefully along the top edge of the paper and notice a bead of paint that builds up on the nearest edge. Reload the brush and repeat the same action, overlapping the bead edge of the last brushstroke. Continue down the paper like this until you have covered the area. Clean up the last bead of paint at the bottom with the end of the brush.

There are many variations of the basic wash and it is worth taking time to experiment. Blend off a wash simply by adding more and more clear water as you proceed down the paper. Blend colours together gradually or sharply to provide sky effects.

Ancient barges: demonstration

I could hardly believe my luck one weekend when I discovered these three ancient sea-going barges moored at low tide in a river estuary. Their dark low hulls and intricate rigging make them a wonderful subject for watercolour. Before painting them, I took some photographs from different angles as I knew these three vessels would make excellent reference material for many future paintings.

Size: 367 × 264 mm/14½ × 10½ in. Paper: T H Saunders NOT 180gsm/90lb. Brushes: Chinese bamboo no. 9, 1 sable, flat sable, Colours used: cadmium orange, cadmium red, yellow ochre, burnt sienna, cobalt blue, Prussian blue.

Stage 1

Draw the composition faintly with an HB pencil. Use masking fluid to describe the thin white lines along the sides of the boats, the odd rope dangling over the water and the anchors on the front of two of the barges. As the sky is quite pale it is possible to over-paint all the rigging details without any fear of the sky disrupting them.

Paint the sky with a wash using two mixtures of paint. First introduce a strip of clear water across the horizon and then blend a mixture of cadmium orange and yellow ochre with a touch of cadmium red into this clear water. Above this apply another mixture of cobalt blue and burnt sienna to merge with the yellows of the first wash. Let this dry before proceeding any further. Put in the strip of dark vegetation on the horizon using Prussian blue with a dash of yellow ochre.

Stage 2

Use a mixture of cadmium red and Prussian blue to paint the dark barge hulls. I never use black as I can

Stage 1

Stage 2

Stage 3

Stage 4

get any depth of colour I need by mixing dark colours. When painting the barge hulls, vary the tone so that there are dark shadows and areas of lighter value.

Stage 3

Work on the masts and sails by using thin washes of cadmium orange and a little yellow ochre for variety of colour. Take great care to keep your brushstrokes absolutely straight when painting the masts. Put in some tiny dots of burnt sienna mixed with cadmium red on the decks of the barges to create detail and interest.

Stage 4

Continue work on the sails and use pure cobalt blue for the ropes that come down from the masts and sails. Put these in with swift sharp strokes using a very fine sable brush. A steady hand is needed to paint the rigging. I find that the easiest way is to swing my arm from the elbow rather like a large compass.

Paint the water surrounding the boats with a wash, tinted with yellow ochre and cadmium orange. Use cadmium red to colour the lower hull of the left-hand barge.

Stage 5 – the finished painting

Stage 5

While the wash of the river is still wet, add the blurred reflections of the barges using Prussian blue and cadmium red. When this is dry paint in the ripples on the surface using a no. 1 sable brush. To paint the old jetty timbers on the left, use Prussian blue and cadmium red to describe the dark areas. Use slow brushstrokes for these parts but quick drybrush for the broken effect of timber surfaces. These colours are burnt sienna, cadmium orange and yellow ochre.

Paint the foreground with a wash, introducing colours while still wet. When dry, paint in all the bits of rubbish left by the receding tide. Take considerable care to place the pebbles and give them shape and colour: merely dabbing away with a brush will not give this effect. Run a wet brush underneath each pebble, causing the paint to run slightly and give an impression of wetness to the sand. To finish the foreground add the chains lying in profusion on the beach, using a strong mixture of cadmium orange and cobalt blue. Vary these colours at will.

Finally complete the barges by scratching in some lines on each hull to denote wooden planks.

College chapel doorway: demonstration

Painting architectural detail is not so difficult as it looks. The most important point to remember is that the preliminary drawing must be very accurate indeed. In this particular case, the left- and right-hand sides of the drawings correspond almost exactly, apart from very minor details of the animals above the doorway.

Size: 254 × 254 mm/10 × 10 in. Paper: T H Saunders NOT 180gsm/90lb. Brushes: Chinese bamboo no. 9, 1 sable, flat sable. Colours used: cadmium orange, cadmium red, bright red, yellow ochre, burnt umber, cobalt blue.

Stage 1

Make a careful drawing of the subject. Make no attempt to add detail or tone but concentrate on proportion and size.

Put in the main background colours with a diluted wash of cadmium orange and bright red. Try to retain the hard edges around these washes. Put in shadows at the top of the doorway with a mixture of cobalt blue and bright red. Use drybrush here to obtain a broken effect that contrasts with the soft wash of the background areas.

Stage 2

To create the effect of rough stonework, use a mixture of cobalt blue and bright red and drybrush at the base of the pillars where grime has collected. Paint the slim pillars with a no. 1 sable brush, holding it lengthwise and slowly dragging it down the paper once. Using the brush in this way gives a far better result than using just the tip to create a light, feathery brushstroke. Use this brush technique with cobalt blue to paint in the arches and details at the top of the right-hand pillar. This is the most critical part of the painting as each brushstroke must work the first time. The painting quickly loses freshness and spontaneity if alterations are made.

Stage 3

Begin work on the inner arch with quick drybrush strokes of burnt umber, bright red and cobalt blue in varying mixes, together with one or two very thin wash marks of cadmium orange mixed with bright red. When dry put in some cobalt blue to give an effect of broken shadow. Underpaint the wooden doors with cobalt blue mixed with a touch of burnt umber. Use the same mixture for the steps, but put in a quick drybrush stroke in the foreground to give a contrast in texture.

Place a very soft hard-edged wash on either side of the doorway. The lower part of this wash is a mixture of yellow ochre and burnt umber, and the upper part is a mixture of burnt umber, bright red and cobalt blue.

opposite:
A monochrome study of the finished painting shown on the back cover. This shows the value of drybrush work in relation to slow wet brushstrokes. It is this contrast that gives this painting its sharpness, even without colour as here.

Stage 1

Stage 2

Stage 3

Stage 4 (*shown on back cover*)

When the paint on the doors has dried, put in the detail using a mixture of cobalt blue and bright red, taking care to let the highlights show through. Use quick drybrush on the lower part of the doors and slow, darker strokes for the upper part to create an effect of shadow and softer detail. The finishing touches to this painting are very subtle. Put thin washes on the large pillar at each side of the door to give rising vertical planes. Place some very thin washes of cobalt blue on the other areas to give extra relief to the stonework. Add a few fine wash strokes to the base of the two columns to show the original colour of the stone underneath the grime. Give body and detail to the wall on either side of these pillars with some hard-edged strokes of burnt umber mixed with cobalt blue. Put in some lines to denote the pointing between the stonework. Lastly, add some clear water to the outer edges of the wash on left and right to bleed them softly into the white paper.

Detail of the doorway shown on the back cover

Special techniques

If used with great discretion, special techniques can greatly enhance a watercolour painting. Here are some that I find useful.

I use masking fluid for fine lines and small areas that are too tiny to paint around. Apply it with a fine brush, a dip pen or even the edge of a knife. Always wash your brush immediately after using masking fluid as it sets quite quickly. After the paint is dry, remove the masking fluid with a soft eraser or your finger.

I keep a pan of ox gall in my paint box to produce dramatic highlights in a wash; a small amount applied with a fine brush to a wet wash disperses the paint with great speed, leaving a clear light area.

Sometimes I dab on wet paint with a sponge or tissue to produce an interesting effect with foliage or clouds. Both sponge and tissue can be used to absorb excess water from a wash or to lift out larger areas of colour. You can apply a flat wash with a sponge rather than with a brush, but this takes practice.

To create a random, stippled effect load an old toothbrush with paint and then pull a comb through the bristles so that the paint splatters on to the picture. Exercise *great* care when doing this.

Use an eraser to lighten an area that is too dark. Make sure the paint is thoroughly dry before you try this.

To create fine highlights on a nearly finished painting, scratch the surface of the paper with the tip of a sharp knife or use a razor blade. Do this when the paint is thoroughly dry.

Use the wooden end of a fine sable brush to mark lines into a wash. This technique is useful for producing blades of grass in the foreground of a picture.

Ox gall applied in the left-hand corner makes paint disperse dramatically.

Left, highlights created by rubbing away paint with a soft eraser and right, made by cutting away thin strips of the paper surface with a very sharp knife.

Scratches made with the point of a sharp knife before the paint has completely dried.

Teazels: demonstration

I discovered these teazels growing amid a profusion of weeds by a wall. They made an interesting subject and a strong contrast to the shadowy mass of growth behind. The planning and execution of this painting was quite different to the others in this book and although the end product looks spontaneous, it needed careful planning.

Size: 254 × 254 mm/10 × 10 in. Paper: T H Saunders NOT 180gsm/90lb. Brushes: Chinese bamboo no. 9, 1 sable. Colours used: cadmium yellow, cadmium orange, cadmium red, yellow ochre, Prussian blue, cobalt blue.

Stage 1

Make a very simple drawing of the stems and four heads. Apply a little masking fluid with a fine brush to the spines.

Stage 2

Make a pale wash from cobalt blue and cadmium yellow and paint in the stems. Mix yellow ochre and cadmium orange and put in a very soft wash on each spiky head. Notice how the colour becomes lighter as it progresses upwards.

Stage 3

When dry, use a fine brush to paint the stems with masking fluid and spatter in more masking fluid over the background areas to create patches of light.

Stage 4

Paint the background with two main mixes of colour. Make the dark greens from Prussian blue, cadmium red and cadmium yellow. Make the light greens from cobalt blue and cadmium yellow. Use a separate brush to apply each colour and work quickly leaving no time for the paint to dry and create hard edges. The wet colours flow into one another to give a loose spontaneous effect. Brush some clear water on the left and right extreme edges of the picture so that the colours fade away into the white paper. When the background has dried, put in a few dark dots of Prussian blue to create shadows.

Stage 5

Put in some dark brushstrokes behind the teazel to give deeper shadows. Mix a lighter green from the same colours and put in markings on the teazel leaves and the sepals at the top of the stem; with a fine brush, flick in some sharp lines around the edge of each teazel to create spikes. Take care not to make these details too dark for their purpose is to bring the teazel into sharp focus against the blurred mass of undergrowth behind.

page 17:
Detail of teazels showing the effective use of masking fluid.

Stage 1

Stage 2

Stage 3

Stage 4

Stage 5 – the finished painting

Words of advice

If you spend a long time on a painting, you may reach a point when it is not quite complete and you are uncertain how you should finish it. An excellent solution to this problem is to hold the painting up to a large mirror to see the reverse image. This is just like seeing a painting for the first time and makes it far easier to be critical. An equally effective remedy is to leave the painting alone for a few days and to return to it after a long rest.

I never use black in any of my paintings as the overuse of this colour is the surest way to kill a picture. It is possible to mix an almost black colour from dark blues.

Do not cut a watercolour painting away from the board too soon after completing work. If you do so it will cockle. I always leave a painting on the board for at least a day to make absolutely sure it is dry.

I advise the use of a putty eraser which does not leave pieces of rubber on clean white paper or attack its delicately structured surface.

When painting indoors with the sun shining directly on to your paper, drape a large white cotton sheet across the window to diffuse and tone down the very strong sunlight.

Conditions for painting outdoors are very rarely perfect. Glare from white paper, hot sun or strong wind are very uncomfortable. Arm yourself with a fishing umbrella, sunglasses, a broad-rimmed hat and a good anorak. All this equipment will make you look formidable but at least you will be able to paint.

When you are pleased with a painting, avoid a large extravagant signature as it can completely ruin the overall effect of the work.

Correcting mistakes

Bad mistakes in watercolour painting are usually irreversible. Here are a few exceptions to the rule.

It is possible to remove an unsuccessful wash by soaking it up quickly with tissues before any hard edges have formed. The success of this depends on the colours used; Prussian blue is a strong dye and this process will lighten but not entirely remove the colour. Cobalt blue is much weaker and may be soaked up, leaving hardly a trace.

Re-soak the areas where the paint has dried and then press tissues firmly against the paper to remove at least some of the colour. If this does not work, scrub the area lightly with a wet bristle brush and then lift out the colour with tissues.

Introduce highlight by rubbing away areas of dry paint with a soft eraser.

These techniques are all useful, but if you apply them too liberally they will cause a painting to lose its freshness.

Other useful pieces of equipment

I use some unusual pieces of equipment in my work. When impatiently waiting for a wash to dry, a hairdryer speeds up the process. Do not hold it too close to the paper or you will blow the water around and create awkward hard edges on the work. On the whole, I think it is best to wait for a wash to dry out naturally.

One piece of equipment I find absolutely essential is a container for my favourite brushes. I made mine from a rolled piece of acetate and two spray-can lids.

opposite:
A few of the basic painting tools that I always have near me when I am working.

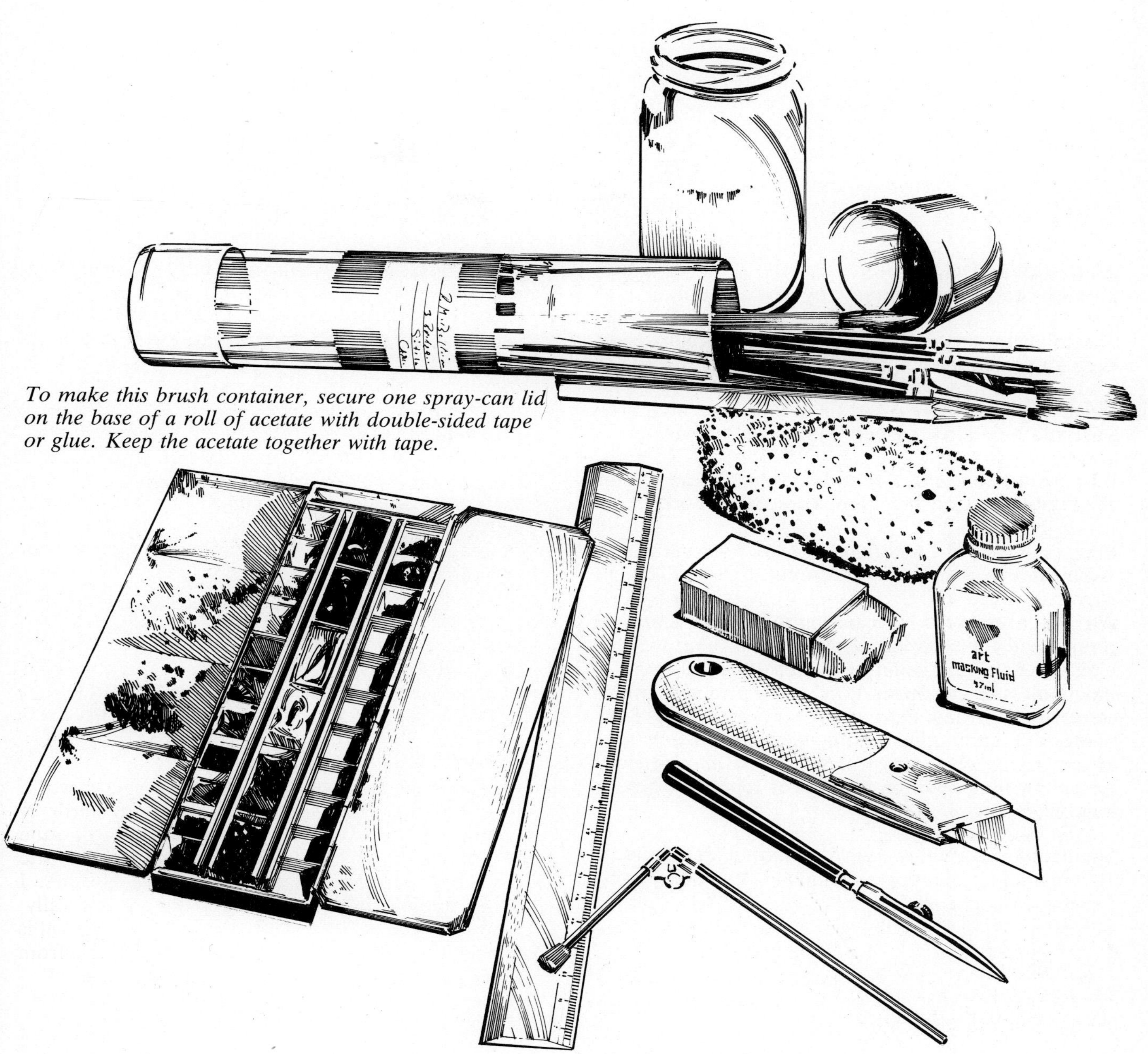

To make this brush container, secure one spray-can lid on the base of a roll of acetate with double-sided tape or glue. Keep the acetate together with tape.

ACKNOWLEDGMENTS
Text, drawings and paintings by Richard Bolton

First published in Great Britain in 1981 by Search Press Limited, 2–10 Jerdan Place, London SW6 5PT.

First published in the United States in 1981 by Taplinger Publishing Co., Inc. New York, New York.

First published in Australia in 1981 by Methuen of Australia Pty Ltd, 31 Market Street, Sydney 2000.

Simultaneously published in London: Search Press.
1. Watercolour painting – technique. 1. Title. (Series: Leisure Arts, No. 9).
751.42′2

UK ISBN 0 85532 440 6
US ISBN 0 8008 6195 7
Aust ISBN 0 454 00303 X.

Made and printed in Spain by A. G. Elkar, S. Coop. Bilbao–12